# A Split in Time
## COMPANION WORKBOOK

How to Write Dual Timeline, Split Time, and Time-Slip Fiction

BY MORGAN TARPLEY SMITH

FOREWORD BY MELANIE DOBSON

# *A SPLIT IN TIME*

# HOW TO WRITE DUAL TIMELINE, SPLIT TIME, AND TIME-SLIP FICTION

## COMPANION WORKBOOK

© 2022, Morgan Tarpley Smith

All rights reserved. Published in the United States of America. No part of this book may be reproduced in any form or by any electronic or mechanical means, including information storage and retrieval systems, without written permission of the author. For more information, address inkmappress@gmail.com

ISBN 978-1-952928-29-1 (paperback)

Published in Pollock, Louisiana, by Ink Map Press

www.inkmappress.com

Cover Design by Victoria Davis

Cover Image (left): Stokkete/Shutterstock

Cover Image (right): Leszek Czerwonka/Shutterstock

The elements of Writing Time-Slip Fiction are used with permission, (c) Melanie Dobson, 2022.

# FOREWORD

## by Melanie Dobson

I've been enchanted with time-slip fiction for years. The mysteries from the past woven seamlessly into a contemporary story. Secrets of much-loved characters that alter the path of a future generation. Themes that bridge time and make us reflect on our own lives in the midst.

All of it inspires me to wonder.

Some people call this type of fiction split time. Others have named it dual timeline. Time-slip simply means taking readers on a journey between two or more time periods.

The name of this genre doesn't really matter. It's the heart of these stories that I love most. The curiosity and hope and, dare I say, magic.

I want to preserve this genre like many of my characters who preserve heirlooms from their ancestors or forgotten stories that beg to be told. And I want to encourage other time-slip writers as they hone the skills and determination needed to write a novel with more than one timeline. Encourage them to dream endlessly about the possibilities.

It's with this same heart that I compiled much of what I've learned about weaving together past and contemporary plots into a book called *A Split in Time: How to Write Dual Timeline, Split Time, and Time-Slip Fiction.* This resource was inspired by my workshop on how to write time-slip fiction, and it was an honor to collaborate with my friend Morgan Tarpley Smith to answer questions from other writers and expand these concepts into a reference for both debut and advanced novelists.

Morgan is a faithful champion of split time. She's spent years studying and marketing this genre, reading voraciously and writing her own stories. Now she has created this workbook along with *A Split in Time* to help writers compile and organize their many ideas.

*A Split in Time* workbook is the perfect companion for writers to brainstorm and outline the essential components of any split time novel including how to develop a compelling character arc, create bridges to the past, and pass critical batons between past and present plotlines. Because critiquing other novels is important in writing this genre, Morgan's companion workbook also contains a sample novel analysis and multiple worksheets so writers can easily analyze time-slip novels on their own.

*A Split in Time* is not meant to be a rule book. It's more like a flight manual for writers on the runway, ready to assist as you takeoff. Once you're airborne, you can spread your wings wide and fly with your story, any direction you choose.

It's a pleasure to join you on this journey!

**~Melanie Dobson**

**The following book is a recommended read as this workbook is a companion to it.**

This workbook is written as a companion to the book, *A Split in Time: How to Write Dual Timeline, Split Time, and Time-Slip Fiction*. It offers an abbreviated look at the material in the book and gives you hands-on worksheets, exercises, and lists to put into practice the concepts, techniques, and advice found in *A Split in Time*. You'll need both the book and the workbook to get the most out of this process.

## A Split in Time:
## How to Write Dual Timeline, Split Time, and Time-Slip Fiction

by Melanie Dobson & Morgan Tarpley Smith

**What are the key elements to writing a time-slip novel? Where do you start in your plot? How do you weave together multiple storylines?**

In *A Split in Time*, time-slip authors **Melanie Dobson** and **Morgan Tarpley Smith** help fellow writers navigate and then master the challenges of writing a novel with two or more storylines. Within these pages you'll find:

· *Thirteen key components for split time fiction*

· *Practical tips on building the time-slip structure*

· *Interviews with bestselling novelists like Lisa Wingate and Susan Meissner*

· *Analyses of multi-storyline techniques*

· *Resources to build compelling split time characters, craft your ideas, and weave together multiple timelines*

**Whether you are a seasoned writer ready for a new journey or a first-time novelist wanting to learn the split timeline format, this workshop-in-a-book provides the necessary skills to weave two or more compelling stories into one time-slip novel!**

# TABLE OF CONTENTS

**SECTION ONE**..................................................................................................1

Introduction........................................................................................................2

Is This Genre Right For You?.............................................................................3

**SECTION TWO**..................................................................................................5

Keys to Write Split Time Fiction........................................................................6

Review Checklist...............................................................................................23

**SECTION THREE**............................................................................................25

Jump-Start Your Split Time Novel...................................................................26

Advanced Questions for Your Story................................................................28

Split Time Novel Reading List.........................................................................41

Comparable Title List......................................................................................43

**SECTION FOUR**..............................................................................................49

Novel Analysis..................................................................................................50

Analysis Worksheets........................................................................................54

**SECTION FIVE**................................................................................................75

Organization & Advice from Authors.............................................................76

Conclusion & Resources..................................................................................80

About the Authors............................................................................................82

# SECTION ONE

## INTRODUCTION

## IS THIS GENRE RIGHT FOR YOU?

"I write (split time fiction) to explore the past and its impact on my own family as well as other families and time periods with my novels." – **Leslie Gould**

"I needed to tell both sides of the story, really get into the heads of those living with the crimes of the past and those dealing with the fallout in more modern times. Writing a dual timeline was the only way I knew to fully explore all sides of the characters and the relevant questions." – **Cathy Gohlke**

"Have a passion for (split time fiction). Don't write it because it's the 'latest' thing. Know that you have a strong story in the past as well as the present. Develop all the characters to the fullest." – **Rachel Hauck**

"I became a dual time writer because for me, there was no other way to tell the *Heirloom Secrets* stories. I wanted the characters, both past and present, to have distinct voices in the story. And I loved the interplay between timelines. I felt like it would do the stories a disservice if they were not set up in a split time structure." – **Ashley Clark**

# INTRODUCTION

## by Morgan Tarpley Smith

I fell in love with this style of novel due to its weaving of past and present. I have always loved history and how I can connect it to myself today. It's perhaps the feeling of not losing our connection to our own ancestral past or that of our country and world in general.

But through fiction we can not only preserve this past but make history come alive for our readers and open their minds and hearts to the important truth that it has to offer us, truth that remains relevant in the present.

I hope the tools, resources, and insight from fellow authors in this workbook help you navigate the challenge of writing this wonderful style of novel. Inside, you will also find three copies of each major worksheet and exercise to allow you to plan up to three split time novels within this workbook.

## WHAT IS SPLIT TIME FICTION?

*Split time novels*, by definition, *consist of two or more storylines.*

In this workbook, we will use the terms "contemporary" and "historical" plotlines to represent a past and present story. The story most current and then one further in the past.

Whether you are a seasoned writer ready for a new journey or a first-time novelist wanting to learn the split timeline format, this workbook (along with *A Split in Time* writing book) will provide the necessary skills to weave two or more compelling stories into one time-slip novel.

# IS THIS GENRE RIGHT FOR YOU?

Writing time-slip fiction requires an incredible amount of curiosity. The kind that almost everyone else, except a fellow writer, will think strange.

**For example**, do you walk into an old house and wish desperately the walls could whisper their secrets?

One of the most important indicators of if this style of novel is right for you lies within the first question:

*Do you enjoy reading novels with both past and present plots?*

If not, this is most likely not the kind of book for you to write.

As writers, we tend to write what we love to read. If you don't enjoy time-slip fiction, I would suggest you evaluate what types of novels you *do* enjoy reading and look into writing within those styles.

But if your answer above was **YES**, the survey below will further determine if this type of novel is right for you.

**Take a few moments to really think through your answers to the following questions. They will assist you in determining if this style is right for you.**

| | |
|---|---|
| Do you enjoy reading novels with both past and present plots? | YES or NO |
| Do you enjoy writing both historical and contemporary fiction? | YES or NO |
| Do you long to understand a decision or situation from years ago? | YES or NO |
| Does discovering a connection between past and present excite you? | YES or NO |
| Do you like to research? | YES or NO |
| Are you ready for a challenge? | YES or NO |
| Can you embrace: 'If at first you don't succeed, try, try again'? | YES or NO |

Maybe you do love to read this genre, but you did not have many **YES** answers above. It may be that you're not quite ready to take the plunge and dive into writing this genre.

Evaluate what genre you should write in based on which one feels right for you now. You can always try something else later on. But above all *write, write, write* and read books about the craft of fiction writing.

If you did answer **YES** to all or most of the questions above, I am thrilled to join you on your journey and help equip you to accomplish this challenge.

# SECTION TWO

## KEYS TO WRITE SPLIT TIME FICTION

## REVIEW CHECKLIST

"With split time, there's usually an object or event which anchors the story. What is that 'thing' that existed in the past yet has impact in the present?" – **Rachel Hauck**

"It is helpful for me to employ a physical connection between the characters such as an object, a place, or a written record like letters in a prayer box." – **Lisa Wingate**

"I used to be a pantser, but when I found split time, I had to change my strategy because of its interconnectivity with real history. Everything needed to fit together in a way that made sense with those historical moments. Now, I tend to plot out the big moments in the story and leave the rest for creative exploration." – **Ashley Clark**

# KEYS TO WRITE TIME-SLIP FICTION

Weaving together two stories into one novel is an exciting challenge, but one that can feel overwhelming at times. While each time-slip story is unique, some of the key components remain the same.

**Below are thirteen elements, compiled by Melanie Dobson, to help direct the structure of your split time manuscript.**

## Components of a Time-Slip Novel

- Multiple Time Periods (Writing Process/Story Structure)
- Contemporary Characters Solving Past Mysteries
- Bridge to the Past
- Compelling Reason to Solve Mystery NOW
- A Past and Present Protagonist
- Different Points of View
- Conflict and Character Arc in Both Past and Present Plots
- Backstory Is Front Story
- *Tell* in Present Story, *Show* in Past Story
- Foreshadow Past Plot through Present
- Passing the Baton
- Mirror Theme/Premise in Past and Present
- Stories Collide Near the End

**How exactly do these key elements play out in a full-length novel?**

In Section Four of this workbook, a split time novel will be analyzed in light of these components, and you'll find Novel Analysis worksheets too, so you can analyze your manuscript and other split time books on your own.

## Multiple Time Periods

A split time novel must have multiple storylines in more than one time period. Some even feature three or four time periods. Most authors weave together a historical and contemporary plot while others have two historical plots or two distinct contemporary plots or more that are set in different years.

How many storylines do you prefer for a split time novel (reading or writing)? Why?

_____

_____

_____

_____

## Writing Process

When it comes to the actual writing of the storylines, each author has their own unique writing process, sometimes even changing their method for each novel.

**Heidi Chiavaroli** always starts her books with the contemporary storyline. In contrast, **Leslie Gould** writes each of her split time novels differently. Most of **Susan Meissner**'s dual storylines have been written simultaneously since she learns about the main characters by actually writing their story. (***Note***: More writing advice from popular authors can be found in this workbook's final section.)

## Story Structure

How you structure the back and forth is up to you, but the following are three common formats to allow your readers to smoothly transition between your time periods:

- *Staccato story*
- *Sandwich story*
- *Sectional story*

The **staccato story** intertwines storylines while switching equally between each one, usually every other chapter.

The **sandwich story** (or what some call *a frame structure*) is a time-slip story where the beginning and end section are usually contemporary and the entire middle contains the past story.

The **sectional story** contains a long section of one storyline and then switches to a long section from the other, weaving it together like the staccato format except readers stay grounded in the past and then the present for longer periods of time.

Any of these formats work well for a time-slip story.

Do you have a preference for one of the three? Why? _____
_____
_____
_____

**Name novels done in each style.**

<u>Staccato</u>
**The Lost Castle** series by Kristy Cambron
**Before We Were Yours** by Lisa Wingate
**Memories of Glass** by Melanie Dobson

_____
_____
_____


<u>Sandwich</u>
**The Nightingale** by Kristin Hannah

_____
_____


<u>Sectional</u>
**The Tea Chest** by Heidi Chiavaroli
**Cousins of the Dove** series by Leslie Gould and Mindy Starns Clark
**A Fall of Marigolds** by Susan Meissner

_____
_____

# Contemporary Characters Solving Past Mysteries

The beauty of the split time genre is that our readers learn what happened long ago through a compelling story instead of dialogue. Not all time-slip novels have a mystery component, but an unsolved mystery from the past will keep readers engaged through the contemporary story.

There are quite a few varying degrees of mystery found within split time novels. Some of these include but are not limited to . . .

- **Echoes Among the Stones** by Jaime Jo Wright – a murder
- **The Forgotten Seamstress** by Liz Trenow – a lost child
- **The Lost Castle** series by Kristy Cambron – three different castles
- **Memories of Glass** by Melanie Dobson – a family legacy
- **The Wedding Dress** by Rachel Hauck – the journey of a wedding dress
- **Heirloom Secrets** series by Ashley Clark – the search for lost loved ones

Elements can also be combined to add extra depth and complexity to a mystery such as what happened to an object (a painting) and a building (historical house turned museum) in **Bellewether** by Susanna Kearsley.

What unsolved mysteries intrigue you? How could you incorporate one into a story idea?

_____

_____

_____

_____

_____

_____

_____

_____

## Bridge to the Past

Usually a token or symbol ties together the past and present in split time fiction. It is a bridge, in a sense, so the contemporary character has something tangible to remind them of what happened long ago.

- *Freedom's Ring* by Heidi Chiavaroli – an antique ring
- *A Fall of Marigolds* by Susan Meissner – a scarf
- *The Story Keeper* by Lisa Wingate – an old partial manuscript
- *The Writing Desk* by Rachel Hauck – a writing desk
- *The Curse of Misty Wayfair* by Jaime Jo Wright – an old photograph
- *The Butterfly and the Violin* by Kristy Cambron – a hidden painting
- *The Dress Shop on King Street* by Ashley Clark – a hat, satchel, and buttons

What physical objects (connections) do you like to see in split time novels?

_____
_____
_____
_____

Which ones would you like to use in your own novels? Why? _____
_____
_____
_____
_____
_____
_____

# Compelling Reason to Solve Mystery NOW

Sometimes the contemporary characters stumble onto the past mystery and sometimes an event prompts the protagonist to search for information, but no matter how the story begins, this mystery thread quickly becomes a pressing matter.

What mystery or mysteries could your protagonist(s) solve? _____

_____

_____

_____

_____

_____

Why does the mystery need to be solved now for our contemporary characters?

_____

_____

_____

What has happened in the present to make this an urgent matter? _____

_____

_____

_____

_____

Just like in a contemporary or historical novel, there must be an inciting incident and a point of no return for the protagonist—a catalyst to jump-start the story and hook your reader.

If you are not sure what an inciting incident or a point of no return are, here are a few recommended writing books:

- ***Plot & Structure*** by James Scott Bell
- ***Writing the Breakout Novel*** by Donald Maass
- ***Guide to Fiction Writing*** by Phyllis A. Whitney

## A Past and Present Protagonist

Instead of one hero or heroine, the split time genre typically has a contemporary and a historical protagonist. These protagonists should want something throughout the novel, and they will do almost anything to achieve their goal. In order for the story to flow smoothly, readers should care deeply about both protagonists and empathize, if possible, with their conflict.

What are possible conflicts for your protagonists? _____

_____

_____

_____

_____

Why should readers care deeply about them? _____

_____

_____

_____

_____

# Different Points of View

Novels are written through the perspective of one or more characters in the first person or third person (he/she) point of view. The key is to show a character's point of view in a way that will capture the reader. For beginning writers, it may be best to try third person at first or one storyline in first person and the other in third.

One approach to test out if you should use a first-person point of view as well as get to know your character better is to write a journal entry, so let us do so now for our main protagonists. If you are undecided which of your characters are your main protagonists, you can do this exercise for each perspective one and see who stands out.

**WRITE A JOURNAL ENTRY about one of the following:** processing a difficult family situation, reflecting on the wonderful day they had, meeting a romantic interest, witnessing a horrible event, or what they wish would happen in their future.

**Character #1 (Contemporary):** _____

_____

_____

_____

_____

_____

_____

_____

_____

_____

_____

**Character #2 (Past):** _____

**Character #3 (Optional):** _____

## Conflict and Character Arc in Both Past and Present Plots

The contemporary protagonist's main external goal is often to find out what happened in the past, but what she discovers should change her internally as well. The past discovery should rock our hero or heroine off their axis and send him or her spinning in an entirely new direction. It will change their present and probably their future.

What past discovery could forever change your contemporary protagonist's life?

_____

_____

_____

_____

_____

_____

_____

## Backstory Is Front Story

The beauty of writing in this genre is that we get to SHOW much of what happened long ago in the historical plotline. Much of the backstory in time-slip fiction is our FRONT story.

Do you prefer split time novels that start with a contemporary or historical storyline? Why?

_____

_____

_____

_____

## *Tell* in Present Story, *Show* in Past Story.

The showing AND telling is a favorite feature of time-slip. We get to TELL part of our story through the contemporary plotline even as we show it happening in the past.

Do you prefer split time novels where the protagonist discovers something new or builds upon prior knowledge or experience? Do you have a preference? Why or why not?

_____
_____
_____
_____
_____
_____
_____
_____

## Foreshadow Past Plot through Present

With writing time-slip, you can foreshadow what's going to happen in the past story by what the contemporary characters find out in their research or what they already know about history.

What are some scenarios you could foreshadow in a split time story?

_____
_____
_____
_____

## Passing the Baton

One of the most effective ways to weave together a split time story is to pass the baton well between the past and present stories. The baton could be weather—a storm might begin at the end of a contemporary chapter and then we pan straight over to a storm in the past. The baton could be similar dialogue or décor or a situation that transcends time. This is not a technique we should use for every chapter, but it is one that helps transition between multiple time periods without jarring the reader.

What are some other ways to pass the baton between storylines? _____

_____

_____

_____

_____

_____

## Mirror Theme/Premise in Past and Present

In this resource, the heart of our stories is referred to as the **moral premise** based on the resource ***The Moral Premise: Harnessing Virtue & Vice for Box Office Success*** by Stanley Williams.

The protagonists in both the past and present plots **AND** the antagonist(s) should wrestle with the same vice and virtue.

One virtue and one opposing vice that transcends time. The protagonist will ultimately choose the VIRTUE and your antagonist will ultimately choose the VICE. But they both should be given this choice.

The moral premise for Melanie Dobson's novel, ***Catching the Wind***, is:

*Unforgiveness leads to a lifetime of regret (vice),<br>
but forgiveness leads to the restoration of relationships (virtue).*

No one else will see our moral premise, but it should be the guiding light of our stories, the focus of our message.

What themes do you enjoy in split time novels? Why? _____
_____
_____
_____
_____
_____
_____

What themes would you like to explore in your novels? Why? _____
_____
_____
_____
_____
_____
_____

What are some negative choices your characters could face? _____
_____
_____
_____
_____
_____
_____

What vices could these negative choices lead to? _____

_____

_____

_____

_____

What positive choices could counter the negative ones? _____

_____

_____

_____

_____

Which virtues could these positive choices lead to? _____

_____

_____

_____

_____

**Now put some of these together . . .**

### *Moral Premise #1*

*(NEGATIVE CHOICE)_____ leads to (VICE)_____,*

*but (POSITIVE CHOICE) _____ leads to (VIRTUE)_____.*

## Moral Premise #2

*(NEGATIVE CHOICE)*_____ *leads to (VICE)*_____,

*but (POSITIVE CHOICE)* _____ *leads to (VIRTUE)*_____.

## Stories Collide Near the End

The stories of the contemporary and past protagonists intersect at some point, usually with a huge collision when the present-day character discovers a secret or something that has affected them personally.

In the end, the past story can be revealed to the present protagonist in different ways. The protagonist could learn the entire truth or just enough to be greatly affected by the past.

What are some ways the past storyline changes your contemporary protagonist's life?

_____

_____

_____

_____

What are some ideas for your storylines to collide near the end (Ex: find object, meet someone, travel somewhere, etc.)?

_____

_____

_____

_____

_____

# REVIEW CHECKLIST

## Common Mistakes to Avoid in Split Time Fiction

- Repeating information in the past and present plots
- A missing token or symbol that bridges the past to the present
- Contemporary characters who don't have a connection to the historical plot
- Contradicting a prior chapter or revealing something not yet ready to be revealed in the contemporary storyline
- Imbalance between past and present plots
- An extensive cast without differentiating the characters
- Neglecting an urgent reason for the contemporary characters to act now
- Forgetting to establish a clear internal journey for the past and present protagonists so they both have to choose between good and evil in their lives
- Rough transitions between past and present
- Discord between the concluding timelines
- No surprise at the end

# SECTION THREE

JUMP-START YOUR SPLIT TIME NOVEL

ADVANCED QUESTIONS FOR YOUR STORY

SPLIT TIME NOVEL READING LIST

COMPARABLE TITLE LIST

"Be clear what the story questions are for both of your main characters and then map the two threads out in detail. Think through what artifacts and metaphors can span the two stories and help connect them. Think through the minor characters in each thread and how you can connect them too." – **Leslie Gould**

"Create unique inner voices as well as appropriate dialect in dialogue for your characters, making certain those voices reflect the two different time periods. Weave both stories in a way that reveals what must be known only as needed. This approach maintains suspense and will lead readers to the 'aha moment'." – **Cathy Gohlke**

"Even though you're telling two stories, one narrator's story will control the pace and drive of the story. Typically, that's the present-day narrator, who is discovering or in some way mirroring the life of the historical character." – **Lisa Wingate**

# Jump-Start A Split Time Novel
## Worksheet #1

Even those who prefer writing as *pantsers* should do a little planning before launching into a split time novel. Here are some basic questions to jump-start your story:

Working Title: _____

Number of storylines in the book? _____

What are the time periods of the storylines (all historical, all contemporary, combination of contemporary and historical)? _____

## **Contemporary Timeline**

Settings: _____

Year: _____

Who is the Protagonist? _____

Protagonist Point of View: _____

What is Her/His Primary Goal? _____

What is Keeping the Protagonist from Obtaining Her/His Goal? _____

_____

_____

# **Past Timeline**

Settings: _____

Year: _____

Who is the Protagonist? _____

Protagonist Point of View? _____

What is Her/His Primary Goal? _____

What is Keeping the Protagonist from Obtaining Her/His Goal? _____

_____

_____

_____

Bridge to the Past (event, objects, etc.)? _____

Story Structure (Staccato, Sectional, or Sandwich)? _____

Story Begins with the Present or Past? _____

# Advanced Questions for Your Story *Worksheet #1*

**Working Title:** _____


Why does your story have to be told through split time? _____

_____

_____

_____

_____

_____


Will your contemporary protagonist already know some information about the past? If yes, what? _____

_____

_____

_____

_____

_____

What is the inciting incident and point of no return for each protagonist?

_____

_____

_____

_____

_____

_____

Why is your contemporary protagonist highly motivated to find out about what happened in the past? _____

_____

_____

_____

_____

_____

How will the contemporary character be forever changed externally and internally by her discovery? _____

_____

_____

_____

_____

Which twist(s) will surprise your reader? _____

_____

_____

_____

_____

How will you stitch up the threads of your story in the end? _____

_____

_____

_____

_____

_____

# Jump-Start A Split Time Novel
## Worksheet #2

Working Title: _____

Number of storylines in the book? _____

What are the time periods of the storylines (all historical, all contemporary, combination of contemporary and historical)?_____

## **Contemporary Timeline**

Settings: _____

Year: _____

Who is the Protagonist? _____

Protagonist Point of View: _____

What is Her/His Primary Goal? _____

What is Keeping the Protagonist from Obtaining Her/His Goal? _____

_____

_____

_____

_____

# **Past Timeline**

Settings: _____

Year: _____

Who is the Protagonist? _____

Protagonist Point of View? _____

What is Her/His Primary Goal? _____

What is Keeping the Protagonist from Obtaining Her/His Goal? _____
_____
_____
_____
_____

Bridge to the Past (event, objects, etc.)? _____

Story Structure (Staccato, Sectional, or Sandwich)? _____

Story Begins with the Present or Past? _____

# Advanced Questions for Your Story *Worksheet #2*

**Working Title:** _____

Why does your story have to be told through split time? _____

_____

_____

_____

_____

_____

Will your contemporary protagonist already know some information about the past? If yes, what? _____

_____

_____

_____

_____

_____

What is the inciting incident and point of no return for each protagonist?

_____

_____

_____

_____

_____

_____

Why is your contemporary protagonist highly motivated to find out about what happened in the past? _____

_____

_____

_____

_____

_____

How will the contemporary character be forever changed externally and internally by her discovery? _____

_____

_____

_____

_____

Which twist(s) will surprise your reader? _____

_____

_____

_____

_____

How will you stitch up the threads of your story in the end? _____

_____

_____

_____

_____

# Jump-Start A Split Time Novel
## Worksheet #3

Working Title: _____

Number of storylines in the book? _____

What is the time period of the storylines (all historical, all contemporary, combination of contemporary and historical)?_____

## **Contemporary Timeline**

Settings: _____

Year: _____

Who is the Protagonist? _____

Protagonist Point of View: _____

What is Her/His Primary Goal? _____

What is Keeping the Protagonist from Obtaining Her/His Goal? _____

_____

_____

_____

_____

# **Past Timeline**

Settings: _____

Year: _____

Who is the Protagonist? _____

Protagonist Point of View? _____

What is Her/His Primary Goal? _____

What is Keeping the Protagonist from Obtaining Her/His Goal? _____
_____
_____
_____
_____

Bridge to the Past (event, objects, etc.)? _____

Story Structure (Staccato, Sectional, or Sandwich)? _____

Story Begins with the Present or Past? _____

# Advanced Questions for Your Story *Worksheet #3*

**Working Title:** _____

Why does your story have to be told through split time? _____

_____

_____

_____

_____

_____

_____

Will your contemporary protagonist already know some information about the past? If yes, what? _____

_____

_____

_____

_____

_____

What is the inciting incident and point of no return for each protagonist?

___

Why is your contemporary protagonist highly motivated to find out about what happened in the past? ___

How will the contemporary character be forever changed externally and internally by her discovery? _____

_____

_____

_____

_____

Which twist(s) will surprise your reader? _____

_____

_____

_____

_____

How will you stitch up the threads of your story in the end? _____

_____

_____

_____

_____

# Split Time Fiction Reading List

**Title:** _____  Author: _____

Setting(s): _____  Time Periods: _____

**Title:** _____  Author: _____

Setting(s): _____  Time Periods: _____

**Title:** _____  Author: _____

Setting(s): _____  Time Periods: _____

**Title:** _____  Author: _____

Setting(s): _____  Time Periods: _____

**Title:** _____  Author: _____

Setting(s): _____  Time Periods: _____

**Title:** _____  Author: _____

Setting(s): _____  Time Periods: _____

**Title:** _____  Author: _____

Setting(s): _____  Time Periods: _____

**Title:** _____  Author: _____

Setting(s): _____  Time Periods: _____

**Title:** _____  Author: _____

Setting(s): _____  Time Periods: _____

**Title:** _____  Author: _____

Setting(s): _____  Time Periods: _____

**Title**: _____ Author: _____

Setting(s): _____ Time Periods: _____

**Title**: _____ Author: _____

Setting(s): _____ Time Periods: _____

**Title**: _____ Author: _____

Setting(s): _____ Time Periods: _____

**Title**: _____ Author: _____

Setting(s): _____ Time Periods: _____

**Title**: _____ Author: _____

Setting(s): _____ Time Periods: _____

**Title**: _____ Author: _____

Setting(s): _____ Time Periods: _____

**Title**: _____ Author: _____

Setting(s): _____ Time Periods: _____

**Title**: _____ Author: _____

Setting(s): _____ Time Periods: _____

**Title**: _____ Author: _____

Setting(s): _____ Time Periods: _____

**Title**: _____ Author: _____

Setting(s): _____ Time Periods: _____

# Comparable Title List

Whether you are considering a traditional publishing route or a self-publishing one, you need to know what published novels are most like yours in subject or theme, etc. and which novels your future readership are enjoying.

One tool to finding comparable titles is the bookshelf of the Goodreads group, *Split Time Fiction That Travels*. I have catalogued hundreds of split time novels under different labels such as settings, era, release year, dual timeline, or multiple timelines, etc. Start by looking at the same settings or eras of your novel and expand from there.

**For: (Working Title)** _____

**Title**: _____ Author: _____

Setting(s): _____ Time Periods: _____

Publisher: _____ Publication Year: _____

Why is this novel a comparable title for your novel? _____

_____

_____

_____

**Title**: _____ Author: _____

Setting(s): _____ Time Periods: _____

Publisher: _____ Publication Year: _____

Why is this novel a comparable title for your novel? _____

_____

_____

_____

**Title:** _____ Author: _____

Setting(s): _____ Time Periods: _____

Publisher: _____ Publication Year: _____

Why is this novel a comparable title for your novel? _____

_____

_____

_____

**Title:** _____ Author: _____

Setting(s): _____ Time Periods: _____

Publisher: _____ Publication Year: _____

Why is this novel a comparable title for your novel? _____

_____

_____

_____

**Title:** _____ Author: _____

Setting(s): _____ Time Periods: _____

Publisher: _____ Publication Year: _____

Why is this novel a comparable title for your novel? _____

_____

_____

_____

**For: (Working Title)** _____

**Title:** _____ Author: _____

Setting(s): _____ Time Periods: _____

Publisher: _____ Publication Year: _____

Why is this novel a comparable title for your novel? _____

_____

_____

_____

**Title:** _____ Author: _____

Setting(s): _____ Time Periods: _____

Publisher: _____ Publication Year: _____

Why is this novel a comparable title for your novel? _____

_____

_____

_____

**Title:** _____ Author: _____

Setting(s): _____ Time Periods: _____

Publisher: _____ Publication Year: _____

Why is this novel a comparable title for your novel? _____

_____

_____

**Title**: _____  Author: _____

Setting(s): _____  Time Periods: _____

Publisher: _____  Publication Year: _____

Why is this novel a comparable title for your novel? _____
_____
_____
_____

**Title**: _____  Author: _____

Setting(s): _____  Time Periods: _____

Publisher: _____  Publication Year: _____

Why is this novel a comparable title for your novel? _____
_____
_____
_____

**Title**: _____  Author: _____

Setting(s): _____  Time Periods: _____

Publisher: _____  Publication Year: _____

Why is this novel a comparable title for your novel? _____
_____
_____
_____

**For: (Working Title)** _____

**Title:** _____ Author: _____

Setting(s): _____ Time Periods: _____

Publisher: _____ Publication Year: _____

Why is this novel a comparable title for your novel? _____

_____

_____

_____

**Title:** _____ Author: _____

Setting(s): _____ Time Periods: _____

Publisher: _____ Publication Year: _____

Why is this novel a comparable title for your novel? _____

_____

_____

_____

**Title:** _____ Author: _____

Setting(s): _____ Time Periods: _____

Publisher: _____ Publication Year: _____

Why is this novel a comparable title for your novel? _____

_____

_____

**Title**: _____ Author: _____

Setting(s): _____ Time Periods: _____

Publisher: _____ Publication Year: _____

Why is this novel a comparable title for your novel? _____

_____

_____

_____

**Title**: _____ Author: _____

Setting(s): _____ Time Periods: _____

Publisher: _____ Publication Year: _____

Why is this novel a comparable title for your novel? _____

_____

_____

_____

**Title**: _____ Author: _____

Setting(s): _____ Time Periods: _____

Publisher: _____ Publication Year: _____

Why is this novel a comparable title for your novel? _____

_____

_____

_____

# SECTION FOUR

## NOVEL ANALYSIS

*The Dress Shop on King Street*
ASHLEY CLARK

## NOVEL ANALYSES FOR YOUR NOVELS

"I try to make all my decisions for the story's good, not my own. My preferences always have to be second to the story's needs. I don't think of myself as a slave to the story though. I am still the master of the narrative. I just choose to make decisions on what is best for the story, not what is easiest or best or preferred by me." – **Susan Meissner**

"To take an idea and a piece of history and an experience and translate it into a book is my favorite part of the process." – **Kristy Cambron**

"I write the story exactly the way you read it. I don't hop back and forth. I literally write it the way it's written in the book. I see it like a movie in my head." – **Jaime Jo Wright**

"I feel like my best writing is when I'm surprised along with the reader. For me, doing too much planning can stifle that process, so I like to leave some room for the story to take on its own life." – **Ashley Clark**

# NOVEL ANALYSIS

## *The Dress Shop on King Street*

## by Ashley Clark

Following is an analysis of the key elements in **The Dress Shop on King Street**, the debut novel of author Ashley Clark and the first in her *Heirloom Secrets* trilogy, but before we break it down, here is a bit more about the story:

> Harper Dupree has pinned all her hopes on a future in fashion design. But when it comes crashing down around her, she returns home to Fairhope, Alabama, and to Millie, the woman who first taught her how to sew. As Harper rethinks her own future, long-hidden secrets about Millie's past are brought to light.
>
> In 1946, Millie Middleton—the daughter of an Italian man and a Black woman—boarded a train and left Charleston to keep half of her heritage hidden. She carried with her two heirloom buttons and the dream of owning a dress store. She never expected to meet a charming train jumper who changed her life forever . . . and led her yet again to a heartbreaking choice about which heritage would define her future.
>
> Now, together, Harper and Millie return to Charleston to find the man who may hold the answers they seek . . . and a chance at the dress shop they've both dreamed of. But it's not until all appears lost that they see the unexpected ways to mend what frayed between the seams.

***A huge thank you to Ashley for allowing me to break down her story like this:***

**Multiple Time Periods**
Ashley's novel spans a range of timelines from 1946 to 1968 with the majority of the historical story set in 1946 and 1952 and the contemporary set overall in modern day (2020) with a glimpse of 1992, 2008, and 2011 woven within. The prologue is set in 1860.

**Contemporary Characters Solving Past Mysteries**
When the novel opens, the life of the contemporary heroine, Harper Dupree, is adrift after she has reached a dead end pursuing a career in fashion. She finds her way back home to a caring elderly woman named Millie, who taught her to sew years before. Millie's lifelong dream is to own a dress shop in Charleston, and Harper is determined to help her, but she does not expect to meet the handsome Peter Perkins or for Millie's past to come calling.

Ashley uses the ***staccato format*** for this story, the chapters moving rapidly between the present and the past with a few instances where there are two present-day chapters or two historical chapters back-to-back. In Chapter 7, Peter's discovery leads his path to collide with Harper and Millie, and he and Harper must work together to unravel the tight-lipped Millie's past.

**A Past and Present Protagonist**
Harper is the main present-day protagonist with Peter as the secondary. Millie is the main protagonist from the past with a charming train jumper named Franklin as the secondary. Millie is still alive in the present scenes, but the contemporary story is focused on Harper's journey.

**Different Points of View**
The contemporary chapters are written from both Harper and Peter's third-person perspectives while the past chapters are from the third-person perspectives of both Millie and Franklin. The prologue is written in third person from the perspective of an enslaved woman named Rose, who we learn more about as the novel unfolds.

**Conflict and Character Arc in Both Past and Present Plots**
The past and present stories are filled with compelling conflict—romance, tragedy, fear, end of a dream, loss of identity, and separation. Harper and Millie both have a character arc to complete.

In the contemporary plot, Harper needs to release her feelings of failure, loss of identity, and the death of a dream. She also needs to learn to look at life as a second chance when plans don't go as she wanted and overcome discouragement from others. Millie has a mirror of this arc in the past as she struggles with the same issues on top of the racial prejudice of the time and the danger she and her loved ones face due to her bi-racial heritage.

In the present, Harper and Millie need each other to complete their individual journeys. Harper's father tells her in Chapter Four that "sometimes you have to look for the next good thing," which becomes integral to both her and Millie's stories.

**Bridge to the Past**
The main bridge to the past surrounds an old, embroidered satchel from the 1860s that contains several mementos of that era including two special buttons that are integral to the story and are referenced within the prologue. This satchel reappears later in the story as do the buttons.

Other bridges are a letter, a red cloche hat, and a vintage wedding dress. I will leave their explanation for when you dive into Ashley's wonderful story for yourself.

**Compelling Reason to Solve Mystery NOW**
Millie is an elderly woman harboring a lifetime of secrets including her heritage as the daughter of an Italian man and a Black woman. As Harper connects more pieces of Millie's past, she wants to help Millie reconcile as much of the past as she can in the present while she is still living.

**Backstory Is Front Story**
The backstory of the past storyline slowly comes out in pieces as the story unfolds and Harper and Peter discover more about Millie's past. The reader, of course, has direct insight into the historical story as these discoveries are brought to light in the present day and then revealed in the past chapters.

***Tell* in Present Story, *Show* in Past Story**
The beauty of split time fiction is that we can SEE the past taking place in real time versus someone in present day TELLING us about what happened in the past or only revealing pieces of the past. In this format, we experience the whole story and move between the timelines seamlessly as more is revealed.

**Foreshadow Past Plot through Present**
In the contemporary plot, we learn early on that Millie has harbored secrets of the past surrounding her bi-racial heritage. Harper and Peter understand her reasons are due to a tragic death and the violence linked to racial prejudice in the southern United States at that time. However, further secrets remain that are foreshadowed throughout the novel that will also affect Millie's present.

**Passing the Baton**
An example of *passing the baton* in Ashley's novel would be at the end of Chapter 23 when Harper admires a gorgeous dress and Millie seems affected by seeing it too, but she feigns any knowledge of the dress. In the start of Chapter 24 though, Millie is wearing that exact dress in the past. Then, back to the present day in Chapter 25, Harper is wondering about Millie's reaction to seeing the dress and what she isn't sharing.

Another example would be at the end of Chapter 19 when in the past Millie and Franklin are sitting on a porch watching the "moonlight dip into the dawn." In the start of Chapter 20 in modern day, Harper reflects that it must have been "the rosy glow of twilight" when thinking about an interaction with Peter.

**Mirror Theme/Premise in Past & Present**
The themes in both past and present center on, but are not limited to, reconciliation, overcoming fear and shame, and forgiving oneself. I'm not privy to Ashley's premise, but I suspect it might have gone something like this:

*Fear and shame lead to brokenness,*
*but forgiveness leads to reconciliation and second chances.*

As a result of each character's choices, whether or not they choose to forgive themselves and others, they either have regret at the end of the story or the restoration of their relationships. In Chapter 32, Peter asks Harper, "... have you considered whether fear—rather than your dream—is what you're holding onto?"

The question makes Harper truly question the role fear plays in her life as well as Millie's. The height of fear for Millie in the past occurs in Chapter 33, and Millie addresses fear in the present-day story in Chapter 39.

**Stories Collide Near the End**
Harper and Millie's stories physically collided with their reunion in the present day at the beginning of the novel, and by Chapter 27, the biggest pieces of the stories start really being stitched together between past and present. However, more secrets are still left to be answered, including how Millie's story creates a true turning point in Harper's life which comes in the end of Chapter 32. Further collision with the past occurs in Chapter 39.

I want to tell you how the past and present stories fully collide perfectly by the end, but you'll have to read *The Dress Shop on King Street* to see how it happens. That being said, both the present and past stories bring us to the dress shop and the restoration of both Harper and Millie's dream. What once was a painful symbol of the past now brings hope for the future to both women in the present.

# *Novel Analysis*
# Worksheet #1

Before you begin working on your time-slip story, I recommend that you read a few of your favorite split time novels (ones that really inspire you) and analyze them, getting to the heart of why you love these particular novels.

**Novel Name:** _____

**Author:** _____

**Publisher & Year of Publication:** _____

## Multiple Time Periods

How many storylines does the novel contain (two or more)? _____

What are the time periods of the storylines (all historical, all contemporary, combination of contemporary and historical)? _____

_____

Is it a Staccato, Sandwich, or Sectional story? _____

## Contemporary Characters Solving Past Mysteries

What is the contemporary protagonist highly motivated to find out about the past?

_____

_____

_____

Is there an unsolved mystery surrounding a murder, a missing person, or a mysterious object (or a combination of several mysteries) for the contemporary character to solve?

_____

_____

_____

## A Past and Present Protagonist

What do the protagonists want and intently pursue throughout the novel? What are the characters' wants and goals that readers deeply care about? _____

_____

_____

_____

_____

_____

## Different Points of View

What point of view is used for the protagonists (both third person, both first person, or a combo of first and third person)? _____

_____

_____

_____

Did you think the point of view choices were effective? Why or why not? _____

_____

_____

_____

_____

## Conflict and Character Arc in Both Past & Present Plots

How does the contemporary character go in a whole new direction and be forever changed externally and internally by her discovery about the past? _____

_____

_____

_____

_____

## Bridge to the Past

What is the token or symbol (bridge to the past) that ties together the past and present storylines? _____

_____

_____

_____

## Compelling Reason to Solve Mystery NOW

Why does the mystery need to be solved now for the contemporary characters? What has happened to make this an urgent matter to resolve? _____

_____

_____

_____

_____

What is the inciting incident and point of no return for each protagonist?

_____

_____

_____

_____

_____

_____

## Backstory is Front Story

Does the novel begin with a past or present storyline? _____

Why is the backstory necessary for the plot to be complete? _____

_____

_____

_____

_____

### *Tell* in Present Story, *Show* in Past Story

What time period is featured in the historical storyline? Is it a well-known one?

_____

_____

Does the contemporary protagonist already have some information about the historical period or the past characters? _____

_____

_____

_____

### Foreshadow Past Plot through Present

How does the contemporary character's research and knowledge foreshadow pieces of the plot in the past storyline? _____

_____

_____

### Passing the Baton

Was the "pass the baton" technique used in the novel? _____

What are some ways the author transitioned between storylines? _____

_____

_____

_____

## Mirror Theme/Premise in Past & Present

What are the main themes (grief, forgiveness, identity, etc.) of the story?

_____

_____

Is there a moral premise? If so, how would you define it? _____

    *(NEGATIVE CHOICE)*_____ leads to *(VICE)*_____,

    but *(POSITIVE CHOICE)* _____ leads to *(VIRTUE)*_____.

What dilemmas do the protagonists and antagonists both face based on this vice and virtue? _____

_____

_____

_____

_____

## Stories Collide Near the End

How do the protagonists wrestle with the moral premise or story theme a final time?

_____

_____

_____

_____

_____

How do the storylines intersect with a huge collision? _____
_____
_____
_____
_____
_____

Which threads and major plot points do the author use to stitch up the novel near the end?
_____
_____
_____
_____

In what way or ways does the historical story change the contemporary protagonist's life?
_____
_____
_____
_____
_____
_____
_____

# *Novel Analysis*

# Worksheet #2

Analyze another split time novel using the worksheet below.

**Novel Name:** _____

**Author:** _____

**Publisher & Year of Publication:** _____

## Multiple Time Periods

How many storylines does the novel contain (two or more)? _____

What are the time periods of the storylines (all historical, all contemporary, combination of contemporary and historical)? _____

_____

Is it a Staccato, Sandwich, or Sectional story? _____

## Contemporary Characters Solving Past Mysteries

What is the contemporary protagonist highly motivated to find out about the past?

_____

_____

_____

Is there an unsolved mystery surrounding a murder, a missing person, or a mysterious object (or a combination of several mysteries) for the contemporary character to solve?

_____
_____
_____
_____

## A Past and Present Protagonist

What do the protagonists want and intently pursue throughout the novel? What are the characters' wants and goals that readers deeply care about? _____

_____
_____
_____
_____

## Different Points of View

What point of view is used for the protagonists (both third person, both first person, or a combo of first and third person)? _____

_____
_____
_____

Did you think the point of view choices were effective? Why or why not? _____

_____

_____

_____

## Conflict and Character Arc in Both Past & Present Plots

How does the contemporary character go in a whole new direction and be forever changed externally and internally by her discovery about the past? _____

_____

_____

_____

_____

_____

## Bridge to the Past

What is the token or symbol (bridge to the past) that ties together the past and present storylines? _____

_____

_____

_____

_____

_____

## Compelling Reason to Solve Mystery NOW

Why does the mystery need to be solved now for the contemporary characters? What has happened to make this an urgent matter to resolve? _____
_____
_____

What is the inciting incident and point of no return for each protagonist?
_____
_____
_____
_____
_____
_____

## Backstory is Front Story

Does the novel begin with a past or present storyline? _____

Why is the backstory necessary for the plot to be complete? _____
_____
_____
_____
_____
_____
_____

## *Tell* in Present Story, *Show* in Past Story

What time period is featured in the historical storyline? Is it a well-known one?

_____

_____

_____

_____

Does the contemporary protagonist already have some information about the historical period or the past characters? _____

_____

_____

_____

## Foreshadow Past Plot through Present

How does the contemporary character's research and knowledge foreshadow pieces of the plot in the past storyline? _____

_____

_____

_____

_____

_____

_____

## Passing the Baton

Was the "pass the baton" technique used in the novel? _____

What are some ways the author transitioned between storylines? _____

_____

_____

_____

_____

## Mirror Theme/Premise in Past & Present

What are the main themes (grief, forgiveness, identity, etc.) of the story?

_____

_____

Is there a moral premise? If so, how would you define it? _____

    (NEGATIVE CHOICE)_____ leads to (VICE)_____,
  but (POSITIVE CHOICE) _____ leads to (VIRTUE)_____.

What dilemmas do the protagonists and antagonists both face based on this vice and virtue? _____

_____

_____

_____

_____

**Stories Collide Near the End**

How do the protagonists wrestle with the moral premise or story theme a final time?

_____
_____
_____
_____
_____
_____

How do the storylines intersect with a huge collision? _____

_____
_____
_____
_____
_____
_____

Which threads and major plot points do the author use to stitch up the novel near the end?

_____
_____
_____
_____
_____
_____

In what way or ways does the historical story change the contemporary protagonist's life?

_____
_____
_____
_____
_____
_____
_____

# *Novel Analysis*

# Worksheet #3

Analyze another split time novel using the worksheet below.

**Novel Name:** _____

**Author:** _____

**Publisher & Year of Publication:** _____

## Multiple Time Periods

How many storylines does the novel contain (two or more)? _____

What are the time periods of the storylines (all historical, all contemporary, combination of contemporary and historical)? _____

_____

Is it a Staccato, Sandwich, or Sectional story? _____

## Contemporary Characters Solving Past Mysteries

What is the contemporary protagonist highly motivated to find out about the past?

_____

_____

_____

Is there an unsolved mystery surrounding a murder, a missing person, or a mysterious object (or a combination of several mysteries) for the contemporary character to solve?

_____

_____

_____

_____

## A Past and Present Protagonist

What do the protagonists want and intently pursue throughout the novel? What are the characters' wants and goals that readers deeply care about? _____

_____

_____

_____

_____

## Different Points of View

What point of view is used for the protagonists (both third person, both first person, or a combo of first and third person)? _____

_____

_____

_____

Did you think the point of view choices were effective? Why or why not? _____

_____

_____

_____

## Conflict and Character Arc in Both Past & Present Plots

How does the contemporary character go in a whole new direction and be forever changed externally and internally by her discovery about the past? _____

_____

_____

_____

_____

## Bridge to the Past

What is the token or symbol (bridge to the past) that ties together the past and present storylines? _____

_____

_____

_____

_____

## Compelling Reason to Solve Mystery NOW

Why does the mystery need to be solved now for the contemporary characters? What has happened to make this an urgent matter to resolve? _____

_____

_____

What is the inciting incident and point of no return for each protagonist?

_____

_____

_____

_____

_____

_____

## Backstory is Front Story

Does the novel begin with a past or present storyline? _____

Why is the backstory necessary for the plot to be complete? _____

_____

_____

_____

_____

_____

_____

## *Tell* in Present Story, *Show* in Past Story

What time period is featured in the historical storyline? Is it a well-known one?

_____

_____

_____

_____

Does the contemporary protagonist already have some information about the historical

period or the past characters? _____

_____

_____

_____

## Foreshadow Past Plot through Present

How does the contemporary character's research and knowledge foreshadow pieces of the

plot in the past storyline? _____

_____

_____

_____

_____

_____

## Passing the Baton

Was the "pass the baton" technique used in the novel? _____

What are some ways the author transitioned between storylines? _____

_____

_____

_____

_____

## Mirror Theme/Premise in Past & Present

What are the main themes (grief, forgiveness, identity, etc.) of the story?

_____

_____

Is there a moral premise? If so, how would you define it? _____

    *(NEGATIVE CHOICE)*_____ *leads to (VICE)*_____,

    *but (POSITIVE CHOICE)* _____ *leads to (VIRTUE)*_____.

What dilemmas do the protagonists and antagonists both face based on this vice and

virtue? _____

_____

_____

_____

_____

**Stories Collide Near the End**

How do the protagonists wrestle with the moral premise or story theme a final time?

_____

_____

_____

_____

_____

_____

How do the storylines intersect with a huge collision? _____

_____

_____

_____

_____

_____

_____

Which threads and major plot points do the author use to stitch up the novel near the end?

_____

_____

_____

_____

_____

_____

In what way or ways does the historical story change the contemporary protagonist's life?

___
___
___
___
___
___
___

# SECTION FIVE

ORGANIZATION

ADVICE FROM SPLIT TIME AUTHORS

RESOURCES

"Study other split time authors and then go for it." – **Rachel Hauck**

"Like any other type of writing, I would say that reading other split time fiction will be helpful. Study how an author tells a successful time split story." – **Heidi Chiavaroli**

"I have a journal that I use for every novel. I will draw my own maps. I will write character descriptions. I will write facts and dates and organize some of my thoughts." – **Kristy Cambron**

"We think about writing a book as one big, long process, but it's absolutely not. There's a moment of first inspiration . . . Then, there's a huge moment of research in which I don't start writing a word until I feel saturated in the world I want to inhabit." – **Katherine Reay**

# How Do We Organize This?

Whether notebooks, journals, binders, Scrivener, or a mass of notes pinned to a giant corkboard, there are a plethora of ways to plot and brainstorm your next split time novel. And in an attempt to figure out what works, the process can be an extremely overwhelming one. I'm speaking from experience. I've tried about all of these and more, and I think I've finally narrowed down what works for me.

The question is: *what do you think will work for you?*

When I first set out to write a time-slip novel I had no idea where to begin, so I naturally turned to advice on blog posts and on the websites of my favorite split time authors.

## Kate Morton's Method

Australian author Kate Morton's split time novels have sold millions of copies and been translated into many languages. She prefers to scribble in multiple notebooks until her storylines are fleshed out, and like Morton, I think the pen in hand and the blank pages of a journal or notebook peering back at me is a fantastic way to dive into a story.

Morton also says when she gets stuck in writing, she'll go to a cozy corner of a coffee shop, notebook in hand, and start writing as fast and furious as she can until the ideas start flowing again and she's back deep into the world of her novel.

## Susanna Kearsley's Method

Another of my favorite split time authors is New York Times best-selling Canadian novelist Susanna Kearsley, who uses another type of notebook system. She uses a three-ring binder with different sections for Research, Timeline/Chronology, Things to Check, Characters, Setting, and more. As Kearsley reads through her primary sources and other research materials, she records her notes and ideas in the binder and references her notes as she writes. Currently, she saves research and documents into a folder on her computer and also has physical copies of research organized in a folder.

Other authors I know use the Evernote app to digitally organize their research or other programs such as Scrivener.

# ADDITIONAL ADVICE
## FROM SPLIT TIME AUTHORS

**PREPARING TO WRITE**

"I don't always write split time fiction, but when I do, it's always because the story just called for it, and I was happy to oblige. For me, split time works best when the story in the past meshes with the story in the present in a way that results in organic relevance. The two narratives need to matter to each other such that the past somehow affects change (either good or bad) when it collides with the story in the present." – ***Susan Meissner***

"I brainstorm pieces of the present and past timelines individually, then I weave the story together in my manuscript to reveal the right information at the right time. I am more of a seat-of-the-pants creator, although I've learned from experience that I need a general roadmap before I set out on my writing journey." – ***Melanie Dobson***

"Focus on a central question or issue that links the two time periods. *What is the connection between the two—the thing that weaves the two stories together?* This thread will create a roadmap—a pathway along which your chosen theme will reveal itself through your characters' experiences and their reactions to those experiences." – ***Cathy Gohlke***

"If I'm not sure what to name (a character) and even if I pick out a name for a historical character, I usually try and check the origins of it to make sure it's not too modern for the era. I want to pick names of that era." – ***Jaime Jo Wright***

**RESEARCH**

"My first priority is the characters. I build their setting around their needs, so it varies from book to book, and I tend to research accordingly." – ***Ashley Clark***

"You may have some people who write the full draft of the manuscript and go back and do research, or they do all the research ahead of time and then they will write the manuscript. I am a researcher as I go." – ***Kristy Cambron***

"All my research is in notebooks. I handwrite everything, and there is no order to it. That way, when I write things down, they become a part of me—more so than if I type them. Not only that, in order for me to find a piece of information, I have to page through the whole notebook, and I stumble over lots of other research . . . It's incredibly chaotic, but it works for me." – ***Katherine Reay***

"When I research, I typically have a research book I'm reading, and I'll highlight with a pen. I'll take notes in a journal next to me of things I might want to remember, but for the most part the type of research I do is kind of like surface research. (It's) more like I have to go with the feel of the area, and the fiction I write isn't necessarily constricted to actual facts. I don't typically use real locations. I don't typically use popular historical events . . . A lot of it does stay in my head when I do my research. I kind of formulate in my brain how that fits into my book so when I go to write the scene it's there." – *Jaime Jo Wright*

"Usually, I allow the story to structure the research rather than letting the research structure the story. I like to begin with a historical secret—something interesting for my characters to explore. Once I have enough research to shape a plot out of that history, I take the story scene by scene to figure out the details." – *Ashley Clark*

"Once I feel pretty immersed in that world and I know how to approach it, I will start tailoring the research to what the story needs. Even at the end of the book, I'm still refining different aspects of the research. I liken it to an iceberg. I need to have the whole iceberg, but ninety percent of that iceberg is going to be underneath the story, holding it up, so the reader believes the ten percent I share with them." – *Katherine Reay*

**WRITING**

"You may have read some split time books in which one timeline is much stronger than the other. I find that they need to be almost written together, and yet, it's really hard to keep your head in those two worlds. I tend to write them together until I can't and then I will focus on one and run it as far as I can go. Then I return to the other timeline, run it as far as I can go before returning to work them together. It's almost like a zipper approach . . . I find the storylines have to talk together or it becomes two independent stories rather than that synergy of the third fabulous story they created together." – *Katherine Reay*

"I really mix it up as far as my approach to writing split time fiction and have done it differently with nearly each one that I've written. Sometimes I'll write it chapter by chapter, jumping back and forth from the contemporary to the historical stories. Other times I've written the entire contemporary story first and then the historical thread." – *Leslie Gould*

"Every novel is different, but usually I start in the historical setting because my plots revolve around an unsolved mystery. Then I ask my contemporary characters why it's urgent for them to discover what happened decades ago . . . Most of us who write split time seem to lean naturally toward a focus on either contemporary or historical. No two novels are structured exactly alike." – *Melanie Dobson*

"If I'm stuck writing, I usually just take a break. I literally go do something else. It might be for a few days, but I kind of let my creative juices reflow and get going." – *Jaime Jo Wright*

"I wrote one storyline at a time, then wove them both together . . . When I allowed myself to stay in one storyline at a time, the words flowed. Once each storyline neared completion, I began weaving the two together, tweaking to reveal the story of the past only as the more modern character came to a point in her journey that it was needed and would have the most impact. The last few chapters were written after that weaving, helping me bring the story to a satisfying conclusion." – *Cathy Gohlke*

"I don't have a writing routine. I literally write when I get an opportunity . . . A lot of my writing is in sprints, so I'll have ten minutes here or twenty minutes there. I will look at how many words I need to get written per week, so if I know that I need to write 10,000 words that week, I just keep picking away at it." – *Jaime Jo Wright*

"So far, I've always started with the contemporary storyline. I don't think there's a right or a wrong way, but I tend to ground myself by starting with the present day. It gives me perspective on where my contemporary characters are in their journey, where they will end up, and how they will change with the help of my historical characters. More often than not, it will also give me a lens in which to better view my historical story." – *Heidi Chiavaroli*

"I'm a completely linear writer—I write the book just as the reader will eventually read it, rather than writing the contemporary and historical stories separately and then threading them together. I think that's partly because I'm more of a discover-as-I-go writer than an intense pre-plotter." – *Lisa Wingate*

## PUBLICATION JOURNEY

"I really believe in writing conferences and writing communities, and secondly, I believe in unpublished writing contests. You're going to gain great feedback, and you're going to gain confidence." – *Kristy Cambron*

"Adaptability is one of the best assets you can have when it comes to pursuing publication because you inevitably are going to face setbacks even if you are the world's greatest writer." – *Ashley Clark*

# CONCLUSION

Hopefully, you have a plethora of ideas running through your mind now to begin a new manuscript or guidelines to rewrite and tweak an existing time-slip story.

I would like to extend a special invitation for you to check out my Facebook group for readers of time-slip fiction, ***A Split in Time Fiction Group***, where we chat about all things split time. And as its companion, I created ***Split Time Fiction That Travels***, a Goodreads group that contains an ever-growing comprehensive list of split time novels organized by labels such as setting, book release year, historical events, and time periods.

I would like to thank Melanie Dobson for writing the foreword for this workbook and supporting this project. I would also like to thank authors Carole Lehr Johnson, Stacy T. Simmons, Carrie Turansky, and Liz Tolsma for viewing a final draft of this workbook. Your insight was invaluable. And thank you all who are utilizing this workbook. *Happy writing*.

# RECOMMENDED RESOURCES

## Writing Books

- ***A Split in Time: How to Write Split Time, Dual Timeline, and Time-Slip Fiction*** by Melanie Dobson and Morgan Tarpley Smith
- ***The 38 Most Common Fiction Writing Mistakes*** by Jack M. Bickham
- ***45 Master Characters*** by Victoria Lynn Schmidt
- ***Between the Lines*** by Jessica Page Morrell
- ***The Forest for the Trees*** by Betsy Lerner
- ***Guide to Fiction Writing*** by Phyllis A. Whitney
- ***How to Grow a Novel*** by Sol Stein
- ***The Moral Premise: Harnessing Virtue & Vice for Box Office Success*** by Stanley Williams
- ***Plot & Structure*** by James Scott Bell
- ***Write Your Novel from the Middle*** by James Scott Bell
- ***Writing the Breakout Novel*** by Donald Maass

## **Online Resources**

- **splittimefiction.com**
- **morgantarpleysmith.com** (recommended reads & split time fiction newsletter)
- **A Split in Time Fiction** Facebook Group
- **Split Time Fiction that Travels** Goodreads Group
- **advancedfictionwriting.com e-zine**
- ***Great Courses: How to Write Best-Selling Fiction*** by James Scott Bell, thegreatcourses.com/courses/how-to-write-best-selling-fiction.html
- ***The Creative Penn*** podcast, thecreativepenn.com/podcasts/
- ***Novel Marketing*** podcast, authormedia.com/novel-marketing/

# ABOUT THE AUTHOR

### Morgan Tarpley Smith

Morgan Tarpley Smith is an award-winning newspaper reporter and photographer in Louisiana. She writes split time fiction and is the founder of *A Split in Time Fiction Group* on Facebook and *Split Time Fiction that Travels* on Goodreads. Besides writing and traveling to over a dozen countries, her interests include hanging out at coffee shops, listening to records, and researching genealogy. She resides in Louisiana with her husband and son.

For more information,
visit www.morgantarpleysmith.com

www.ingramcontent.com/pod-product-compliance
Lightning Source LLC
Chambersburg PA
CBHW051807100526
44592CB00016B/2605